Enchanted Eloquence

By S.M. Brooks

For Grampi,

Who always believed that my artistic soul

could do anything I set my mind to.

You were right.

Viscera

Cold as fire, hot as ice,

she's temptation, vice, and

naughty, not nice.

Red Riding Hood

Blood red lips lift into a wolf-toothed grin,

her childlike hand tucking her prize

into her basket alongside the others,

the hoard of organs squelching in delight at their latest edition.

The eyeball seemed to widen under her gleeful stare,

despite its muscle and nerve connections being severed.

Turning on her heel, she stalked back into the darkened wood

whilst donning the last piece of her wicked disguise,

because who would ever suspect the

innocent young woman in the ruby hood?

Captive

"Will you walk into my parlor?" said the spider to the fly

The satin of her skirts rustled in the eerie silence as

her boots clicked across the wooden floors.

With stars in her eyes and a smirk on her lips,

she fixed the drink daintily before handing over the chipped teacup.

Her unwitting guest accepted with a grin as he sipped the poison.

A loud crash of breaking glass,

followed by the harsh thud of his body hitting the floor.

How easily he got caught in her web.

Wraith

Pure as snow, rich as blood,

hard as crystal, thick as mud.

Soft supple flesh weaved over a dark, rotting shell

she plots your demise from her dungeon cell.

Arrival Of The Gods

Hazy minds and bright wide eyes
watch lightning strike across the skies.
Bolts of fire, strong and white-hot
wash away my foolish thoughts
A crash of thunder drawing near
makes me smile, for Zeus is here.

Underworld

Most girls grow up wishing for Hercules

to come and rescue them from their sad lives.

Me?

I yearned for Hades,

wishing that he would present me with pomegranate seeds

and passage to the underworld.

Nightmares

All I see are lonely nights and

all I hear are screams,

I'm sorry, for you just entered

my deadly dreams.

Seasons

Some girls are summer heat,
daisies, strawberries, and sunshine.
I'm fresh falling snow,
eyelashes tinged with frost,
moonlight, and hot chocolate.

Crown

Wildflower crowns are more precious than silver and gold.

They do not tarnish,

instead cycling through the natural circle of life.

Budding.

Full bloom.

Withering.

And once bestowed with a new floral braid,

Rebirth.

Man & Beast

Prince Charming is nothing more than a daydream.

A man with facets of both the huntsman and the wolf is rawer.

More real.

Ying and yang.

Both gentleman and beast.

One-dimensional personalities are dull and unremarkable.

Unless the prince can become the dragon he set his eye on slaying,

he can stay in his ivory tower.

Poison Garden

Ivy crawling over a trellis.

Flowerbeds of belladonna and Dracula orchids.

The heady scent of wild roses invading the senses.

Hidden from the outside world, I lay among the overgrown weeds.

Hours of solitude spent within the grounds of a secret garden.

A simple treasure.

Siren

Seafoam, iridescent pearls, glittering scales.

Sleepy-eyed sailors succumb to the lure of her sweet siren song.

They're helpless to her call as she drags them beneath the waves,

silencing them for eternity with her watery kiss.

Written Whisper

Feathered quills churn out sweet correspondence,

always to be sealed with a kiss.

A few spritzes of poisoned perfume are the perfect finishing touch.

Seductive whispers topped off with delicious death.

Such is the way of love.

Let's Get Lost

Why do people always feel the need to beat the labyrinth?

Rounding each corner with the expectation of making it to the center

then racing towards the exit ruins the fun.

Why rush the journey?

Allow yourself to get swept away in the magic of dead ends.

Who knows?

You might find something extraordinary.

Ice Queen

Icy wind swirls through my hair,

leaving frosted tips in its wake.

My fingers are numb.

The chill so cold it burns my blood.

Dressed in only a thin sheath,

I relish the feel of my body pebbling with goosebumps.

Covering up is not an option.

I wait for Jack Frost to take me.

Death Sentence

Wincing against the slightly bitter taste,

I pop another aril onto my tongue.

Only six remain…

Why stop halfway?

Another pomegranate seed falls past my lips.

May Hades whisk me away forever.

Cottage Core

Corn brooms,

well-worn quilts,

a fire on the hearth.

The cozy cottage keeps my mind warm and lazy.

Steal Me Away

The crunch of fallen leaves underfoot

breaks the shuddering silence of the forest.

A harvest moon bathes the path in an eerie orange glow.

Yellow eyes blink out from beneath a feathered brow,

the snowy owl looking on from his perch high above.

Take me, Goblin King.

I would move the stars for you.

Midnight Paradise

Laying back on moonlit sand,

watching stars shoot across the dark sky.

A salty breeze whips around,

chilly as it feeds off of the crashing waves.

Alone in my solitude,

I breathe in the crisp air.

The empty beach at night is far greater than any tropical paradise.

Shatter Me

A sheep in wolf's clothing is your disguise;

Hard, wild, fierce.

Allow the fur pelt to be shed away.

There is pleasure to be found in being broken.

Lift Me Up

Floating on her back on a moonlit lake,

the stars twinkle above her,

casting their milky reflection upon the placid water.

The heavy gown she wears bears down on her,

the weight trying to sink her.

Flexing her shoulders gives her wings release,

their black feathers creating buoyancy beneath her.

Her wings would always lift her.

Wolfen

Long silken fur.

Intelligent amber eyes.

Sharp fangs peeking out from beneath a wide, strong maw.

Grand paws bounding quickly over the forest floor.

Howling up at the moon, his voice growing louder the fuller it waxes.

Willing to do anything for the good of his pack.

Majestic creature.

King of the forest.

Mountain Majesty

Snowcapped mountains flood into a wonderous array of hues

as the setting sun lowers beneath the frosted peaks.

Marvelous magenta, pearlescent pink, glorious gold, outrageous orange.

Twilight may bring with it darkness,

but it also heralds in a kaleidoscope of color.

Utterly enchanting.

Slipping Away

Do not waste a second watching the sand pour within the hourglass,

for every precious moment spent staring

is a moment less that you are not living.

Alpha

Coarse attitude,

looking down on others,

believing themselves better,

and taking what they want are not traits of an alpha.

This is a poor attempt to bolster their ego and show dominion over their peers.

A true alpha will provide for their pack,

cherish those with omega status,

and protect their flock at all costs.

Yearning

Watching from a mountain high
as dragons glide across the sky.
Oh, how I wish that I could soar
and shed my humanity forevermore.

Reflection

Magic mirror on the wall,

who is the fairest one of all?

Not she of silken hair and wealth,

nor the one with perfect health.

Top hats and waistcoats don't make the man,

neither pallor of duskiness or golden tan.

A martyr may be revered or shunned,

while certain saints may sin,

open your eyes, and look beyond

for true beauty is found within.

Knowledge

Trust the crippled old woman,

her glass jars filled with natural herbs and poultices.

The wisdom she holds was lost to time.

Though not modern,

Its healing properties are abundant.

Heartfelt

I don't need rubies, rings, or gold

to make my dark heart soar.

A single rose means more to my soul

than jewels and gifts galore.

Treat Me

Instead of love letters,
write me dark poetry
and haunting piano compositions.

Magic Lesson

As the hedge witch picks her mushrooms,

sit silently and wait

for her to speak and teach you

how to find a mate.

A sprig of rose she offers,

for a chance at love,

the bark yew for strength,

a feather from a dove.

The potion that she mixes

turns a sickly shade of green,

Cause forcing love upon another

is undeniably mean.

If you drink the tincture

your head will start to fog.

Your hands and feet will slowly numb,

your mind thick as a bog.

The witch will watch your turmoil

quietly with glee,

a lesson of not forcing love

she bestowed upon thee.

Recognition

Open your mind to dancing bear cubs pirouetting through the forest,

faeries trapped in mason jars masquerading as fireflies,

and mermaids transforming into manatees once caught in sailor's nets.

Magic is all around you,

if only you put on your rose-colored glasses to see it.

Power Of Submission

She may consent to using whips and bonds

but at the end of the day

it is her that holds all of the power.

You may dominate her,

but you will never tame her.

Sinful Pleasures

Ice to freeze,

heat to warm,

oil to massage,

soft wax to form.

Lace may abrade

and leather might sting,

but silk will soothe most everything.

Trifecta

Gentle girl of curl and comb,

fierce-hearted woman who fights tooth and bone,

wizened in age and all that is known.

Thus is the cycle of maiden, mother, and crone.

Nature's Beauty

Take time to revel in the beauty Mother Nature gifts us.

Stop to smell the fresh blooms of spring.

Bask in the warmth from the summer sunlight.

Admire the charm of falling autumn leaves.

Catch snowflakes on your tongue with the first flurry of winter.

Façade

Platinum hair and azure eyes

make for the most deft disguise,

hiding sharpened fang and claw

til prey is captured in her maw.

Desolate

I wish upon a star to fly

to the castle in the sky.

Upon exploring the unknown,

I mourn to find myself alone.

Trust

Do not be frightened if she lets you in
enough to receive her scratches and bites.
That she bequeaths them to you at all indicate that
she trusts you with her vulnerability.

Transgressions

In the shadows

wrapped in a satin sheet,

you will hear her whispers

of wicked sins and

dark promises.

Bewildered

She could not wrap her head around

his demand that they leave the Wendy-bird alone.

They were only welcoming her to Neverland.

It was all in good fun.

After all,

they were only trying to drown her.

Oceanic Wonders

The conch shell at her ear

whispers soft temptations of

lazy days sitting in the shallows,

while she searches the horizon

for any sign of a tail fin or trident.

Capitulation

Do not mistake her willingness

to play your dark games

as a sign that she is weak or inferior.

She sets aside her alpha crown for those whom she trusts

to guide her into sweet sin.

Frigid

Invoke her wrath and
she becomes ice,
her frozen scepter tossing you out
into the night.

Predatory

She is a fox, bold and sly
gazing with her amber eyes,
watching him until the day
she chooses to feast upon her prey.

Delectation

She would simper to the gentleman

and moan for the monster.

Cara Mia, Mon Cher

A love like Gomez and Morticia

would be the ultimate bliss.

Best friends.

Pet names.

Unafraid to show affection.

Unapologetically themselves.

Bloom

She is a rose;

Mystique in a name,

beauty in countenance,

strength in a stem,

protected by thorns.

Sides Of A Coin

I need someone unafraid to throw me against the wall and

ravage me with wild kisses,

then in the blink of an eye can morph into refinement and

shower me with featherlight touches

and quietly breathed endearments.

Rendezvous

Take me on a silent midnight walk
through an old cemetery,
holding hands through wrought iron gates
and stealing kisses in the shadow of mausoleums.

Ringmaster

Black and white pinstripes and wool berets,

she fits right in at Parisian cafes.

When dusk gives way into the night

she leads the circus of delight.

Chat Noir

She was a black cat.

Many were too scared to cross her path

due to ill-spoken rumors.

Those who were able to look past the stigma,

she granted with a life of unending friendship.

Familiar

Humans can be fickle, shallow brings

but a familiar will guide you,

companionship, and love until the end of days.

Vicious

Do not taunt the maiden.

The beast inside of her can breathe fire

and bring you to your knees.

Ruin

With venomous claws

and opium laced kissed

she could make men crumble like dust

Sentinel

Most girls have fairy godmothers

who would create gorgeous wardrobes full of gowns

and turn pumpkins into carriages.

She had a guardian angel

with wings black as pitch

who sang songs of battle in her ear.

Pipe Dream

Come to me upon a dark steed,

Offering to make all my nightmares come true.

For what is considered daydreams to most,

my blackened soul wishes to view.

Blanche Neige

With poisoned comb and corset tight,

she tried to kill me out of spite.

Plans fouled by friends until one night

I accepted an apple, just one bite.

Locked away as seasons passed

inside a coffin made of glass.

Years of my life, I did miss

whilst waiting long for true love's kiss.

Command

Lace the corset tighter, dear, until I'm gasping deep for air,

then use your blade to cut the strings and wrap them in my hair.

My back may arch, my hands will tense,

my mind will leak all common sense.

As I fall into that euphoric place,

the hazy bliss of my subspace.

Forgotten

Crumbling ruins.

The skeleton of a once grandiose mansion.

An abandoned baby grand.

I elate at the sound of ghostly fingers

dancing across the keys.

Each room a new adventure.

Kindred

When you find someone whose darkness

matches your own,

hold on tight and don't let go.

Toeing The Line

There is a fine line between pain and pleasure.

Do not let the fear of crossing it ruin your fun.

Never Grow Up

You're never too old to stop hunting
for messages in bottles
or proof of wood nymphs in the forest.
Use the eyes of your inner child to
discover a whole new world.

It Takes Two

With a sinful smirk and sultry glance

I shall lead you in this dance.

A twirl, a spin, then arabesque

will lay the innocence to rest.

Chest to chest and thigh to thigh,

our bodies succumb to the high.

Nip and lick and sigh and moan,

fingers explore while bodies groan.

Head thrown back, throat on display,

I offer myself to you, come what may.

Fangs extend, a thirsty bite

harkens the music of the night.

A drawn-out sigh of pleasures spent

calls for sinners to repent.

I will not regret the choice

to give my desires a loud, proud voice.

Criminal

Emerald eyes and scarlet lips,

creamy skin, and luscious hips.

Curly hair of raven's wing,

innocent of not a thing.

Seducing men with no regard,

she pleads the fifth, guilty as charged.

Crown Me

While your enemies play checkers,

become a chess master and create a checkmate.

Mosaic

There is beauty in broken things that have been painstakingly pieced back together again.

Radiant

Even spiderwebs are dazzling in the bright rays of morning light,
dewdrops glistening off of the iridescent strands.

Portal

A small part of me will never be too old

to knock on the back panels of wardrobes

and look for the one book on the shelf that opens the secret door.

Bouquet

Don't bring me bouquets of carnations and baby's breath.

I long for bundles of bleeding hearts, black calla lilies,

, and lady slippers.

Lost Girl

You can find me at the end of long winding staircases
and twisting tunnels in the secluded library,
lounging in a rocking chair with a storybook of fairytales
from faraway lands.

Fatigued

Do not allow yourself to become jaded

from life's little treasures.

In hindsight,

that hug or smile may be all you needed

at the time to pull you out of eternal darkness.

Dangerous

When love is poisoned,

you need to draw upon every ounce of inner strength

to cut away the dark bonds and free yourself

before it drains your soul of light.

Regret

As children, we always wish to grow up quick,

to shed our juvenile skins and fall into

a world of sophistication and grandeur.

As an adult, I am unable to express how much I regret

not going with Peter Pan to Neverland

while I still had the chance.

Impression

Who is this monster wearing my skin?

You may not always recognize your reflection,

but each is a facet of your true self,

some yet undiscovered.

Reminiscence

On a walk towards the woods one autumn day,

twelve-year-old me was convinced she saw

a tiny blue fairy with holographic wings

hovering mere inches from my face.

Hours spent looking for possible bugs with human-like appendages

no larger than my pinky nail

and trying to make sense of what I saw,

I concluded years later that there was no answer.

The impossible is real

if your mind is open to receiving it.

Give Chase

Follow the stag with the luminous horns and shock white pelt.

He will not lead you astray,

even if you lose sight of him for a bit.

Trust the guardian of the forest.

Hunted

The wind whispering through the trees brings with it an uncanny feeling,

spectral fingers teasing my nape.

The ghostly presence cocoons me with warmth,

temporarily allowing my mind to forget the danger.

The crack of a branch snapping as a booted foot treads ever closer.

I must not forget.

Snapping to attention, I jolt forward with a burst of energy.

He will never stop hunting me.

Unlocked

The snick of the skeleton key twisting in the lock

was both a warning and a victory,

the door creaking open to display the darkness beyond.

Perhaps it was meant to stay hidden.

Lucifer

Swathed in flames with hellhounds bounding at his heels,

he pours his darkness toward you,

ready to leash you in chains like Cerberus.

Would it be so bad to give in to the devil,

when he looked like an avenging angel dressed in shadows?

Fallen

Smile sharp enough to cut glass.

Eyes glinting like garnets in the firelight.

A halo just crooked enough to foreshadow danger.

Wings of sable feathers explode from golden skin.

Do you take the hand of the angel?

Shibari

Bright silken fibers knotted over pale, supple flesh

creating a feast for the eyes.

She was a canvas, his masterpiece.

Erotic yet artistic.

Tantalizing.

Bait

Other girls were pansies,

cute and bright and soft.

She was a Venus flytrap,

cunning, calculating, yet oddly beautiful.

Patiently waiting

for an unsuspecting insect to flutter to its doom.

Noxious

My mind is infected with toxic thoughts and doubts

that eat me away from the inside out.

Escape

Whisk me off to hidden alcoves

away from prying eyes.

Kiss me hard and touch me soft,

the scent of my arousal wafting about.

Fire & Brimstone

I dance amongst the hellfire

and pirouette to heaven's light,

desire escapes my charred soul

wafting into the night.

Gothic

Poe gifted me a beating heart,

while Shelley's monster roamed the dark.

Bronte allowed me to escape to moors wide,

and Stevenson taught me to embrace my Hyde.

Reverie

As I nestle down amongst the furs,

my mind drifts off to dream of

sharpened blades, windy cliffs,

and wild wastelands.

Bambi

Fawn toned skin and bright wide eyes,

with a clumsy sense of grace,

she was the Bambi of his heart,

innocent of face.

On unsure legs, she saunters near

to reach his outstretched hand,

with faith and lust and treason in mind,

her hunter will soon understand.

Send-Off

As music from the violin surrounds her mind and swells,

she glides through her last night of Earth,

for tomorrow she descends to hell.

Curio

The cabinet of curiosities draws me in,

locked behind glass, each trinket within.

A magic wand, a skin-bound book,

the turtle shell, and the captain's hook.

A tiny pair of fairy wings,

an antique amethyst set ring.

With careful hands I reach for the lock

when startled by the chiming clock

ringing out for all to hear,

warning the witching hour is near.

Beast Of Prey

The most eye-catching animals in nature all hide a secret.

They sting harder than the grotesque ones.

A bioluminescent jellyfish with all the colors of the rainbow

will not think twice before stinging you.

The vibrant rings of a coral snake are attractive

until their venom pulses through your bloodstream.

Perhaps under the makeup and fashion,

humans are the same.

Down The Rabbit Hole

Follow the white rabbit without reserve

and you may we rewarded

with a magnificent adventure.

Lip Balm & Waterlilies

On the journey of love,

kiss every frog along the way.

You don't know when you'll stumble across

a secret prince.

Merry Go Round

The pretty painted horses of a carousel may seem innocuous enough

but will trap you into a never-ending loop of monotony

if you forget to leave the saddle.

Sprite

Lolita's innocence mixed with a hatter's madness.

An unexpected combination of virtue and lunacy.

A companion for Puck.

Rip Tide

When depression sets in,

I fight against the flood of self-directed animosity,

lest I become lost for eternity.

Toxic

A garden of poison flowers grows,

helped by the turmoil she seeks to sow.

You may pray the Lord your soul to take,

but your essence she'll trap, to bend and break.

Enter

A door stands in the middle of the silent wood,

all alone in a clearing.

Circling it shows nothing behind it,

but when opened it swings on rusted hinges

to showcase a miasma of swirling clouds.

Do you walk through it?

Gelding

Warriors on golden steeds

can give the princess what she needs,

but I'm drawn to the mare of night,

tempting me with dark delights.

Murky

Fog blankets and misty forest paths

place images of phantoms within my grasp.

Vaudeville

As feathers dance across her skin
The boa weaves a song of sin.
A necklace of pearls keeps things demure,
while the mask of lace remains obscure.
Stockings sheer and corset tight
get slowly shed throughout the night
Some may consider the show grotesque
but she embraces her burlesque.

Ice Play

Surrounded by hoarfrost,

her mind screams for release,

her desperate cries lost on the winds

and he runs the ice along her skin.

Begging

Her lips swollen and bruised,

she pulls against her chains

frantic for another taste.

Aphrodisiacs never felt so good.

Punishment

The satin tie across her eyes
obscures her vision, and her cries
of touch me, tease me, grope me, please me
tumble from her lips, a sweet surprise
as she begs for another rise,
not one, not two, but three.
Palm meets flesh but she can't see,
anticipation come to thee,
flesh turns from pale as snow to rosy skies
as she's thrown over his knee.

Debasement

Being obedient is smiled upon

but you don't know true fun until you misbehave.

The punishment could be divine.

Pixie Play

Lounging on toadstools and tuffets is a great way to spend a day before flying off into the night to join the fireflies at play.

Miscreant

Royal balls with kings and queens may make for clever talk

but strange tea parties with rogues and rebels will give others reason to squawk.

You may pick the royalty and the grand soiree

but I will take a bash with charlatans any other day.

Hollow

There is always more to see

in the hollow of a tree.

Insects crawl and build a hive.

Owlets feed until they thrive.

Fox cubs nap curled into a ball.

Raccoons kits, fluffy and small.

So always take a peek and see

what wonders wait to appear to thee.

Somber

I have always been enthralled

with dilapidated ballrooms and hallowed halls.

Somnolent

Those who warn against pricking a finger on a spindle
clearly underestimate my craving to sleep and dream for years on end.

Explore

Takes me on dates to hidden caves

and secret grottos.

Marauders

The sight of black sails on the horizon don't give me pause as it should. Instead, anticipation grows as the skull and crossbones sigil drifts into view.

Resting Place

Stroll with me along the moors

where secrets come to hide,

amongst the swampy bog-like ground

lay spirits of those who've died.

Rebirth

You may try to shatter her

but like a phoenix

she shall rise from the ashes

and be reborn stronger than before.

Threat

I'm anger and hatred, callous and vain,

they come to try and end my reign.

With a rage to rival the blistering sun,

what doesn't kill me better run.

Harlequin

The straight jacket tightened; the bonds strapped in well

to keep her in imprisoned within her dank cell.

A spritely young woman with harlequin grin,

she imbued executions with a dash of sin.

Her gun she did shoot, made her mallet a toy

in an effort to show off for her princely clown boy.

She'd get down to business, there'd be time for play after.

You can't have slaughter without laughter.

Worthy

Only those who could cut down the hedge of thorns

she built around her heart

would be worthy of her;

mind, body, and soul.

Toxicodendron Radicans

She was poison ivy,

causing an itch in your soul,

redness to come to the surface of your skin,

making your heart swell,

and causing difficulty breathing spreading her essence.

Moondance

She dances beneath the silver full moon,

a vixen of the night.

The way she sways and shimmies

brings a fiendish delight.

Gold Dust Woman

Floaty dresses and granny boots,

with long black shawls for miles,

From beneath her wide-brimmed hat,

she smirks her gypsy wiles.

Answer The Call

Inky skies call to me the way the tide meets the shore.

I yearn to float into their heights, untethered forevermore.

Phantom

Underneath the milky starlight
a silhouette appears from the darkness.
Moonlit skin and obsidian hair,
her blushing body completely bare.
You become captured in her thrall.
You blink and she's gone.
Did she ever really exist at all?

Ownership

Onyx binds and silver rings

Are meant for heathens whose hearts do sing.

Metal tipped leather, my brain it does holler,

for I have done much to earn my collar.

Pirate

The crescent moon lights up the isle
grinning like a Cheshire smile.
A vast dark stretch of endless sand
drowns the tides once shore meets land.
No warning called, his blade does skim
along my neck, attentive of skin.
With care given to teasing, not hurt,
I'm spun around in arms, alert.
A smirk creeps up as I embrace
the rogue swashbuckler as my fate.

Hurricane

She was chaos.

Anarchy followed in her wake,

spreading out a stormy fate.

She was calm, a timely sigh

as she hovered in the eye.

Pandemonium made her heart alight,

turmoil and discord make everything right.

Tossing her wrath out, enough to break bone,

she sat upon her hellish throne.

While demons do reign, the world she'll transform

with her everlasting storm.

Carnival

Cotton candy floss and overpriced games,

giant stuffed bears, and men who eat flames.

Thrill rides, snacks, and mirrored halls,

carny calls, and climbing walls.

Bearded ladies and men of steel,

stollen kisses atop a Ferris wheel.

Shouts of glee and anguished cries,

around each corner a new surprise.

Sweet Lies

Meet me atop the train car,

slick in the twilight rain.

A dangerous game to some,

but to play was worth the gain.

Clothing soaked through from the wetness,

warm hands will stifle the chill.

Passion tumbles from clumsy tongues,

the night gets darker still.

Losing your heart to another,

no inhibitions rise

as you pray and hope and beg

for them to tell you sweet lies.

Croon

Her siren song does cripple

as she flaps her leathery wings

to bring her closer to you darling,

as she begins to sing.

Visions of lust are immoral

but vital to the succubi.

Pretend that what she serenades

is just another lullaby.

Temperance

If they can't weather your storms
then they don't deserve your sunshine.

Defender

The monsters under your bed were never your enemies,

they were your guardian angels,

keeping you safe from the night's horrors.

Without A Mane

Just because someone presents as a lion
doesn't mean they are not cowardly.

Oust

Evicting someone from their home is

more difficult than finding a new renter.

Before you let someone take up residence in your heart,

vet their credentials thoroughly.

Suffer

Sticks and stones can break their bones

but where's the fun in that?

The guillotine brings much more joy,

or perhaps a metal bat...

Phantom Facade

Masks come in many styles,

be it feathered, jeweled, or lace.

Sometimes the boldest masquerade of all

is when someone can hide their true face.

Cultivation

As she sat with her tea

she gazed out the window overlooking her garden.

Four dull grey tombstones sat beneath the bright sunlight,

washed out despite the brightness of the day.

Hmm.

Perhaps the soil was not rich enough.

She would need more human compost if

she wanted her body garden to grow.

Venin

The pastry was crumbly and bitter.

Too bad he was too high off of opium to notice.

She smirked demurely as she sipped her tea.

By the time the belladonna set in,

it would be too late for him.

Poor unfortunate soul.

Aria

Her voice was like a nightingale,
tremulous and high.
With syrupy tone and honeyed words
she sang the lullaby.
Each note that piped out through the air
sliced along their life threads.
By the time the song was done
they would all be dead.

Snip

Beware the crone with scissors
who hunts for new red thread,
for if she snips your lifeline
your soul shall join the dead.

Out Of Reach

A case of lethologica is fascinating indeed,

Until you lose your train of -

Uh.

Um.

The thing.

You know?

Awaken

Mr. Sandman brought me a dream,

one I wish I could forget.

Of demon cries and bright red eyes,

I only wake up once I die…

Or do I?

Cry

Her tears fall wet and heavy,

white tinged pink with blood.

For each new teardrop staining, the snow

joins the garnet flood.

Tonic

Each potion is a puzzle,

its composition art.

Too bad the elixir is missing the piece

to mend a broken heart.

Unlucky In Love

You should hope that Cupid isn't still in training
when you get shot by his arrow.

Primitive

My soul has been so far lost on many occasions

when I desired for nothing more than

joining the Wild Hunt,

spending the rest of my days flying across the skies

in pursuit of raw pleasure.

Honorable

Better to be honest and hated
than disingenuous and beloved.

Chance

If you could spin straw into gold

at the expense of the gold being fools,

would you?

Hoarfrost

Winter ravaged the flowers,

their petals tipped in frost.

Leaves curl and die,

their roots far too dry,

til spring they shall stay lost.

Lacking

Whenever you feel that you're not enough,
remember that two-bite brownies exist.

Immorality

I would rather explore each of the seven deadly sins
than force myself to exhibit the seven holy virtues.

At Dusk

Cobblestone streets come to life

once the gas lamps are lit.

Silent strolls become wild parties,

for rogue royalty befit.

Contraband

If something is labeled forbidden,

it tastes just a little bit sweeter.

Immersion

Unless he's willing to drown

in the darkest depths of your soul,

he's not the one.

Heady

Her arousal is intoxicating,

her prey getting drunk off her lust.

Refuge

Find someone who can give you all the security of a teddy bear
while keeping the grizzly just below the surface,
waiting to pounce.

Cure

Don't be afraid to let those around you
comfort you when you feel broken.
Friendship and love are the best medicine.

Solo

There is a distinct difference between being alone

and wanting to be left alone.

It is possible to be mated yet want solitude.

Ire

Beware her roiling temperament.

At any moment her sky could turn

to storm clouds and

her morning glow to lightning.

Euphoria

She danced upon moonbeams
while dressed only in starlight.

Nestled

Cradled to your chest so tight,

tuck me in and kiss me goodnight.

Elysian

Petals bathed in early morning dew.

Fog blanketing the meadow.

A swallow sings its song,

perched high among the branches of the aspen grove

while wild rabbits hop through the underbrush.

Serenity.

Enclosed

She built the moat around her heart
to protect against unwanted invaders.
If you prove your worthiness,
she may lower the drawbridge.

Dawn's Dance

Waltz with me amongst the weeping willows

at the rise of dawn's first light.

All the fae will watch in awe

and chitter with delight.

Warrior Princess

Depending on how you treat her,
she could be either cherry blossoms or
chariots ready for battle.

Lingering

Echoing strains of the violin
floated through the haunted halls.
A lovesick melody for what once was.

Choose

When given the options of a comforting favorite

or an un-walked journey,

take the unfamiliar option.

Adventure awaits.

Honorifics

An adjustment of title remains to be seen,
don't call me princess when I am the queen.

Fortitude

Beach glass starts out sharp
but over time gets tumbled soft
by crashing waves.
Discovering true beauty takes time.
Be patient enough to let it flourish.

Cultivation

Consider a seed when fostering

your family, friendships, and relationships.

Without being nurtured, a seed is just that.

It has the potential for growth and to bloom

but with no special treatment

It remains stagnant.

Envisage

I shall never stop dreaming

of wyverns flying overhead.

Enchanted forests feel more real

than tossing and turning in my bed.

Leviathan

Armored scales,

eyes dark as pitch,

a scorpion's sting,

powers of a witch.

The fire sits beneath her breast

waiting for its cue.

Mouth made for spitting fire,

she'll be the judge of you.

Evil Queen

Heart of fire,

gown of lace,

she's unafraid to show her face.

Gaze of lust and

dance of sin,

she'll end this game

secured a win.

Fretful tremors,

widened eyes,

they watch her with her deft disguise

which she sheds, trophy in hand:

Snow White's liver.

Now *she's* the fairest throughout the land.

Immortal Romance

Hold me tight to your chest as

we kiss in satin-lined coffins.

Morality

She was not meant for pageantry and falsehoods.

Bold hearts, honor, and loyalty were what she admired.

Mastery

She never considered herself a bleeding heart
until she cried when met with the art
of his Adonis-esque face.

Slumber

Nothing is ever as it seems

when Morpheus guides me through my dreams.

Passion

Last night I learned to tango
while Eros took the lead.
With each caress and teasing word
my body felt more free.

Not Out Of Reach

Why swim with dolphins

when you can dive with mermaids?

Adoration

If they don't worship your soul,

they don't deserve your body.

Lush

Tantalizing kisses over pulse points,

stolen caresses in public

and whispered promises of what's to come

would bring her to her knees.

Longest Night

As winter turns the world to white,

hold me tight on solstice night.

Halcyon

Can you calm inside my head?

I'll invite you to my bed

where you joust my thoughts so vile.

Triumphant.

Maybe you could stay awhile…

Asphyxia

The vines wrapped tightly 'round my neck

to keep me at your call and beck,

have flipped effect and turn me on

driven by a heart so wan.

Au Naturel

Velvet gowns and satin sheets

feel nice upon the skin

but feel much better taken off,

your flesh exposed to sin.

Lush

Strong as marble,

cool as ice,

I'm drunk off you,

my forbidden vice.

Sacchariferous

Bathe me in milk and honey,

all inhibitions retreat.

Come join me in the tub, my dear,

you'll have a feast to eat.

Everlasting

Flowers bloom and leaves do fall
as seasons go and stay,
but one thing that will never change-
my love won't melt away.

Carnivorous

A dangerous, lithe creature

with stripes of orange and black,

the tigress doesn't hesitate

to choose you for a snack.

Pack

Your pack is what and who you make it.

Vampire Kisses

Lips red from being nibbled on

by long and sharpened fang,

swollen up and tender,

for him, her lifeblood sang.

Rebirth

If you strip down my defenses

and leave me raw and bare,

I'll treat you to a secret glimpse

of the phoenix sleeping there.

You may think that you have me

too weakened for this earth.

It's sad that you forget, my dear,

my power of rebirth.

Grotto

Love me behind a waterfall,

our heartbeats the only sound

not drowned out by streams of lust,

my soul becomes unbound.

Coquette

A chaste kiss for the lady,

a rough one for the tramp.

For me, my darling, I'll take both

as befits a sultry vamp.

Possession

The feathering of touches
run up and down my spine,
a silent declaration of proof
to match his words "you're mine."

Peep Show

It's hard to keep the beasts at bay
whilst lounging in her lingerie.

Lair

With blindfold on and ankles bound
I'll lead you to the underground
where I'll keep you in my cave
and teach you how to misbehave.

Contemptible

With silken skin and unstrained lust

she begs and pleads to gain your trust

to play games that are filthy,

where consent is a must.

Disillusioned

Euphoria gains and climbs and swells

like the chime and ring of bells

until it reaches the highest peak…

Why does the aftermath appear so bleak?

Incandescent

Her mind was phosphorescent,

her dreams luminous.

Point Of View

I refuse to be cast as the villain

just so you can be viewed as the hero.

Supernova

She shines far too bright
for them to dull her light.

Pet

Call me kitten and

make me purr.

Priceless

She was a diamond:

Multifaceted.

Blazing radiantly.

Tough.

The most precious gem.

Solivagant

With starlight and moonbeams as my guide

I traverse the streets aimlessly,

observing the lazy town.

Misstep

If her mind isn't overwhelmed with emotion

to the point where she's unable to think,

you're doing it wrong.

Haunting Me

Madness stalks my mind

the way a panther pursues its prey.

Melancholia

Like Ophelia,

she was willing to float down the river of her sorrows,

heedless of drowning.

Perilous

Those who dare disturb my slumber

better have damn good reasoning.

Clockwork Consciousness

Her mechanical heart grew weary,

it's rusted cogs fighting to keep on ticking.

Without proper care, it has begun to seize,

the gears grinding closer to a halt each day

no one reached out to grease it.

Hero

Find someone who makes you feel like Hercules,

giving you the strength to conquer the world.

Envelop

When my demons open their arms to embrace yours,

you'll never be rid of me.

Dormancy

Hearts don't break,

they simply go dormant

until another can awaken them.

A Shade Of Grey

Dark does not equate to evil.

Someone facing more trials and tribulations

may have had to learn to be a little more maleficent to survive.

Cosmic

Make love to me beneath the Milky Way
and dance with me upon Saturn's rings.

Sorrowful Shepherdess

Mary had a little lamb

whose fleece was stained with blood.

She tried to wash him in the lake

but lost him in a flood.

Query

If giants climbed a beanstalk

from their castle in the clouds,

where would they end up?

Assured

Wear your confidence as comfortably
as you wear your own skin.

Dauntless

Don't buy me a drink.
If you want to impress me
buy me a book so we can
embark on its journey together.

Wishing Well

You are never too old
to throw a penny into a wishing well
and yearn for your heart's desire
to be delivered to you,
tied up with a bow.

Sabaism

Don't stare at me with stars in your eyes
and expect me not to worship your darkness.

The Shallows

If you only look skin deep,

you will mistake beauty

for having no beast.

Simple Pleasures

Instead of flowers and fancy restaurants,

help me build a pillow fort

to watch horror movies from within.

Profile

I enjoy long walks through the forest

and overthinking memories from a decade earlier.

Growth

Like a lotus blooming from the mud,
she faced adversity before she could flourish.

Sky High

Having your head in the clouds

is just a sign that your mind and soul are far too free

to be brought down to earth so easily.

Consumed

Like a forest fire that rages through the brushlands,

her soul flames scorching and swift,

her passion consuming everything in her path.

Midsummer

Cotton candy skies call for

late evening sandcastle building,

trips to ice cream parlors,

and stolen kisses under the pier.

Magical

I'm not champagne and caviar,

I'm fairy wine and lembas bread.

Cretinous

Ignorance is believing that

just because something isn't visible to the naked eye,

makes it irrelevant.

Prequel

Every villain is an anti-hero

if you take the time to learn their story.

Galaxy

Upon comet tails, I ride

with the man in the moon,

side by side.

Universe

If I could stroll amongst the constellations

I would play fetch with Sirius,

drink from the big dipper,

and hunt with Orion.

Miniscule

An ephemeral moment
may produce the greatest memory.

Interpret

I will never be an open book.

If you want to hear my stories,

you have to put in the work

to read my pages.

Debauchery

Violation of the mind
and exploration of the senses
can be a truly wondrous thing
if shared with your soulmate.

Wild Animal

Don't assume my beast was tamed

if she's been quiet for a while.

She's just regenerating her strength.

Unending

Nothing is ever over until

the last petal falls.

Barbaric

Unless he can drag

the wildness from my soul to the surface,

he's not the one.

Ecstasy

Penetration of the senses can be sublime

when shared with a partner most divine.

Pied Piper

She can charm your demons out with her ministrations.

If you are unable to reciprocate or pay for her service,

consider your soul forfeit.

Odyssey

The more difficult the bridge is to cross,

the more rewarding the destination on the other side.

Drained

Be unafraid to salt the leeches from your skin

so they can stop draining your soul.

Lion & The Lamb

I crave both savagery and serenity.

Fanciful

If you look at me with those wolf eyes

you should expect Little Red to come out to play.

Safeguard

Protecting your heart is harder than
guarding the most precious treasure on earth.

Astonishment

May you find harmony in innocence and hellfire

if you peek into Pandora's box.

Converge

Phantoms flock to her

like vultures to carrion.

Repression

Your manacles can't hold her down
when she is determined to fell a titan.

Final Rest

As I freeze over and
my mind starts to drift
I pray to Hades to
please take me swift.

Revelry

Kiss me hard and grip me tight,

all wrong becomes right on Mischief Night.

Torment

Some people wear their pains like a badge of honor,

easy for all to see.

Others cocoon it deep in their soul.

Murder Mittens

You may call her kitten and make her purr

but do not forget that she can

hiss and unleash her claws at any time.

Vanguard

Let me be your north star to
guide you home in the darkness.

Refreshing

My mind became intoxicated with thoughts
of rain-drenched meadows and petrichor.

Swell

Don't just splash around

when you can make waves.

Escort

I would shatter my soul into hundreds of radiant pieces

and eject them into the sky to

create a constellation that can lead you back to me.

Deficient

A library without a rolling ladder
just doesn't live up to the dream.

Tiny Pleasures

Get excited by small things that may seem insignificant.

The glow of fireflies over the meadow.

Summer giving way to fall.

The smell of the ocean drifting over the coast.

The bright orange light of a harvest moon.

Feline

Who needs fur stoles

when shoulder cats exist?

Desolation

I am easily entranced by

bats in the belfry,

crumbling stone,

and cries of sanctuary.

Menagerie

My mystical menagerie would be filled with:

fluffy fennec foxes,

elegant unicorns,

glorious peacocks,

warrior wolves

friendly sloths,

snowy owls,

daring dragons,

big cats of every variety,

and playful otters.

Pursuit

She was just a girl who was
willing to chase the blue light of the moon
throughout the night.

Poe

She was Annabel Lee,

unable to escape the beating of a heart beneath the floorboards,

yearning to share a masked dance with death,

and chasing the raven nevermore.

Raider

Billowing black sails on the horizon made her heart beat faster,

not out of fear but excitement.

How long had she waited for this day…

Veiled

Silver filigree framed her eyes,

shining bright with lust in the light of the chandeliers.

To be unknown for even just one night

was bliss.

Trapped

Watched over by ravens and mourning doves,

she lay slumbering in her glass coffin.

Too bad her mind's eye could see everything as if from above,

borrowing the eyes of the guardian great horned owl.

Her closed lips fought against her frozen body to scream.

Blue Blood

She wasn't made for glass slippers.

She paired her ball gowns with converse

and nails painted black.

Petulant

Tinkerbell was so sassy because

Peter Pan was too difficult to deal with.

Lost Boys can't be guided home

no matter how many neon signs light their way.

Unsolicited

She required no formal invitation

to go masquerading

with her master for the night.

Anesthetized

Swirling shadows attacked her mind,

numbing all sane thoughts

on her descent into madness.

Diminutive

It is humbling to think and ponder about the power the moon holds over the tides.

Villainous

Girls from Kansas may shine bright like the sun

but wicked witches have more fun.

Inadequate

Having the ability to make you feel special isn't enough
if they don't take pride in your pleasure.

Ignite

Find someone who can set your mind ablaze

like a meteor shower in the night.

Architecture

The chemical composition of her soul was made up of

elfin beauty,

magical musings,

and orphic wonder.

Coalesce

Her spirit liked to mingle with madness
and dance with dark desire.

Roaring 20s

Whisk me away back to the days

of crooning jazz singers

and illicit speakeasies.

Captain

She may let you sit at the helm for awhile

but don't forget who owns the throne.

Burnt

Upon golden wings, she sails toward the scorching sun,

heedless to the fate of Icarus.

Gypsy In My Soul

I'd run away with a Romani caravan if given half a chance.

Bewitched

She cast her spell on charlatans and vagabonds,

willing them to overthrow the queens and kings

for the good of the land.

Stable

Friendships forged from ironclad bonds
will stand the test of time.

Lounging

She holds her pretty parasol

as she moon-bathes at the edge of the lake.

Beacon

Paper lanterns lift into the sky

carried by a winsome wind.

Stars, suns, and messages to loved ones

adorn the shades,

each a wish for the future.

Belittling

It was humbling to lay beneath the meteor shower, watching as each shooting star falls toward the earth.

Infusion

Thick dark lashes danced along cheekbones,

delicate as butterfly wings.

Snowflakes alit upon them,

their melt mixing with tears.

Juvenility

Wishing on dandelions and
coloring chins with buttercups
brings to mind a childhood
gone far too fast.

Play

Playing in tidepools and

swimming out to sandbars

are golden memories from times long past.

Elfin

If one day she awoke to the

peaks of her ears having grown pointed,

she would rejoice and be ecstatic with wonder.

Promenade

Her dancing slippers were worn and mud-stained from nights spent dancing among the aspen groves.

Fantasia

Escape to a place where mountains can sing,

where night is unending,

and horses have wings.

Concealed

The truth sits hiding in plain sight,

waiting to break free from her tiny moue

and set the world topsy turvy.

Demoness

Onyx horns sprouted from her wild mass of curls,

curving back before jutting towards the sky.

Racing

She chased the white rabbit between the birch trees,

determined to find his rabbit hole so

she could follow him to Wonderland.

Compose

Spectacles perched upon her nose,
she allowed her mind to rage
through the tip of her feather quill,
urging words to jump off the page.

Explore

Take me to forbidden temples and
wander with me throughout somber caverns.

Volcanic

Smoke swirled through her mind,
tending to her lava-hot thoughts
until she was ready to let them erupt,
scorching everything in her path.

Suffocate

If you play with fire,

you will undoubtedly get burned eventually,

but the smoke will annihilate you long before.

Ignite

To signal the start of their amorous game,

the petals of the rose went up in flames.

Toy Soldier

The aroma of fir trees and sugarplums

send my mind scampering to dream of nutcrackers

and mouse kings.

Seelie

Through the bright clearing until you go and turn east,

you stumble upon the fairy feast.

Don't eat the food no matter how tempted,

lest you become trapped in the realm unexempted.

Pose

Elfin of face with an aquiline nose,

her countenance soft and perfect for pose.

He was stripped down and bare with a heart full of trust

as he raised an artist's eye and his worn paintbrush.

Goddess

If Aphrodite could be comfortable in her curves,

so can you.

Barren

A mind is an empty canvas

waiting to be painted with hopes and dreams.

Tumultuous

The sleepy hollow called to both her contentment and chaos.

Suppression

No one believed her sapphire eyes were
capable of hiding such maleficent lies.

Insight

Ancient scrolls and massive tomes

have much magic to impart

if only you're brave enough to break the seal

and dive in from the start.

Torpedo

Wading in a bit at a time was never her way.

She always chose to dive in at the deep end.

Patience

Caught in a riptide,

her mind churned with unease.

It was the calm before the storm.

Waiting for the lightning to strike was torture.

Doe

On clumsy legs just like a fawn
she turned herself toward the dawn,
saddened that the night was gone.

Gallant

He was protective of her,

though he urged her towards courage.

Don't speak.

Act.

Repose

Frost blanketed valleys glowed white

beneath the moonlight,

their wildflowers losing their fight

to stay alive.

No Surrender

She was a fantast who refused to conform
to your idea of reason.

Fantastical

Magic is all around you

if only you're willing to open your eyes to it.

Un-halting

Grasp each precious moment while you can

for Father Time waits for no one.

Big Bad Wolf

What big eyes you have,

wide and bright to drive me mad.

What big ears you have

to listen to my aural salve.

What big teeth you have,

smile too tempting to leave me sad.

What full lips you have

to make me feel all kinds of bad.

Mislead

Appearances are most times deceiving.

It takes a special person to see that

beauty is the beast.

Dense

Animals do not let the weak lead the pack.

Why do humans?

Exotic

Everything is alien until you study it enough.

Unfettered

She would consume the poison

if it meant her soul would be free.

Monotonous

Never wanting to explore your surroundings
is the equivalent of being stuck in a snow globe:
A small shake brings a moment of joy
but once the snow stops falling,
you're back to being static.

Voyeurism

Moss covered angels presided over
their wicked waltz in the moonlight,
the only spectators to their clandestine delights.

Barbaric

Throw me over your shoulder and
steal me away to your dark lair.

With Bated Breath

I'm still waiting to be bitten by a vampire.

Hear me, Dracula?

I'm not getting any younger.

Foretaste

Arctic breath teases the hair at her nape,

causing her skin to erupt into a field of gooseflesh.

The anticipation of what's to come

a delectable torture in its own right.

Nihility

Staircases to nowhere in the middle of the forest

are both mysterious and entrancing.

Do you chance a climb to oblivion?

Dogged

Monsters nipped at her heels

as she ran through the midnight woods.

She dared not look behind her,

lest she trip and fall on a gnarled root.

She feared if they reached her,

she might give in to them and go willingly.

Orchestral

She listened as the wolves howled a moonlit symphony,
both alluring and warning of untold dangers.

Ebbing

The clockwork ground to a halt inside her,

her body going limp.

If only someone would turn her key…

she thought as her mind was lost to oblivion.

Disconnect

When her reflection in the mirror

did not match her movements,

she knew it was time to run and hide.

Apparition

The creak of the swing as it moved
by phantom limbs shatters the silent stillness.
The reflection in the puddle below gives way
to the long-gone child at play.

Creature

The beast that stalks the fields at night

calls upon your fight or flight.

Your body starts to tremble despite

assuring yourself it's all bark and no bite.

Enchanted Eloquence

She was wild thoughts,

abundant dreams

impossible fantasies,

and enchanted eloquence.

She could not be confined.

Acknowledgments

I've never done this before, so this might be an interesting little blurb! Thank you to Nana for keeping my secret, giving me input on cover designs, and fueling my love of fairytales from a young age. You always encouraged my love of reading, letting me stretch our funds for school book orders book fairs, and I can't thank you more for that. Thank you to Grampi for never failing to believe in me and always making it clear that I could reach the sky if I tried. I'll always be your little girl.

Mom- you had no idea that I was doing this but I know you'll keep me on your shelf with pride and show me off to people like you always do. Thank you for always being proud of everything I accomplish. Heidi- you let me send you nonsensical words thrown together and gave me your full support, helping me with my pen-name, titling some of these poems, and you never stopped cheering me on. You don't know how much I appreciate you. Becky- I miss you more! You were so encouraging of my creativity ever since meeting me and you never balked at my wild ideas. Ashley- I don't care that you don't like poetry! You're being included in this! Grade 7 and going strong on the friendship train! I know it's not the debut book you were expecting, but it's what you get. Deal with it! Sheila, Dar, Spencer, Gary… I know that none of you had any inkling this was coming but I thought of all of you while writing and I'm hoping you like the finished product. Lastly, thank you to anyone who is willing to give me a chance by picking up a copy of this book. Words cannot express how much it means to me that I'll be on someone's bookshelf.